MW00915677

DARK GALLERY

PENDERGASTIAN ARTWORK

891

CHRIS ROYAL

Copyright © 2016

All rights reserved. No part of this book may be reproduced, stored in a retrieval system, or transmitted in any form or by any means, electronic, mechanical, photocopying, recording, scanning, or otherwise, without the prior written permission of the artist/publisher.

Permission:

Preston & Child characters copyright © 1992 -2016 by Splendide Mendax, Inc. and Lincoln Child. Used with permission.

Disclaimer:

All the material contained in this book is provided for educational and informational purposes only. No responsibility can be taken for any results or outcomes resulting from the use of this material. While every attempt has been made to provide information that is both accurate and effective, the author does not assume any responsibility for the accuracy or use/misuse of this information.

TINY'S BAIT & BAR

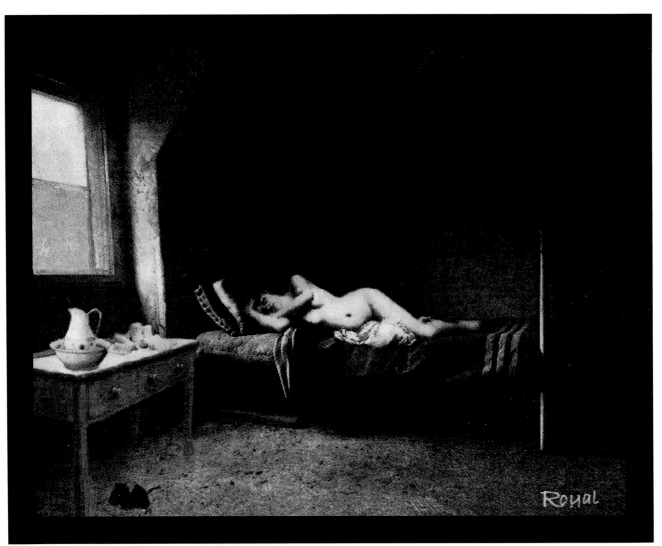

THE BLACK FRAME

SPANISH ISLAND

SLAPPY RIDES ALONG

THE CLOCK

LIGHT READING

WREN

A FITTING END

TRACK RABBIT

RISE OF THE MOLE PEOPLE

THE TOOTH BOX

WAITING FOR HELEN

THE LOCKED BRIDGE

© C. ROYAL

A BURNING PENDENT

LURKING HORROR

JUST A NUMBER

MAAAHHH !

MOVIE PROPS

STEEL WALLS

FROM THE DEPTHS

A LAST SUPPER

MOUNT STROMBOLI

THE ICE LIMIT

GUTTERSNIPES AT PLAY

GUTTER SNIPES

LANG'S LAB

A BABY MAMMOTH

SMITHBACK'S DISCOVERY

ALBAN'S ARRIVAL

WHISPERING DEATH

SALT & RUST

INCITATUS

ALBAN'S RAMPAGE

LOST SON

HAPPIER TIMES

ACID TEST

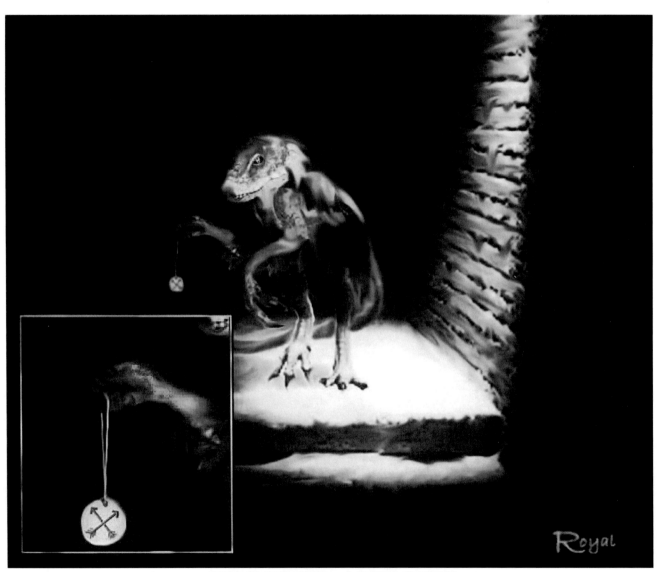

CROSSED ARROWS

DUC CHUC

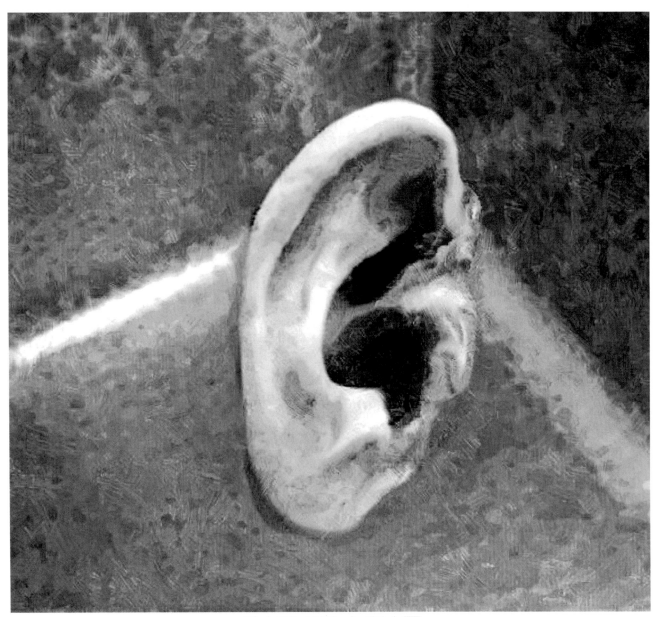

EAR IN A VAT

HALLUCINATIONS #1

OVER-COOKED PASTA

HALLUCINATIONS #2

CHRISTMAS ON RIVERSIDE

A FAMILY PHOTO

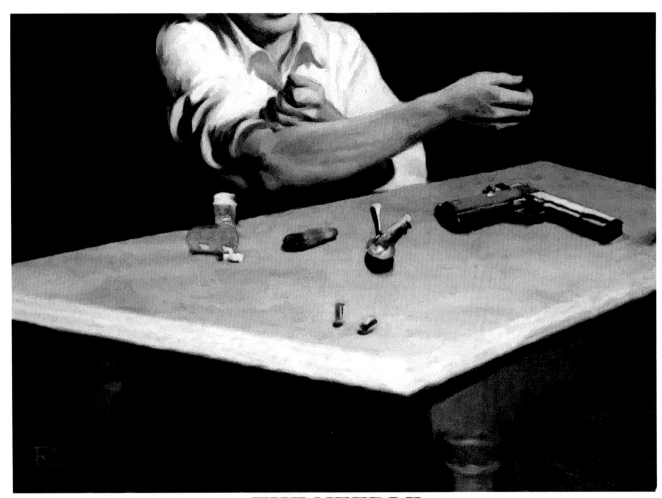

THE NEEDLE

"AVE, FRATER!"

A BLUE STONE

ABSINTHES

DEATH OF THE '45'S

A TIP OF THE HAT

MONSIEUR BERTIN

STRANGER ON A TRAIN

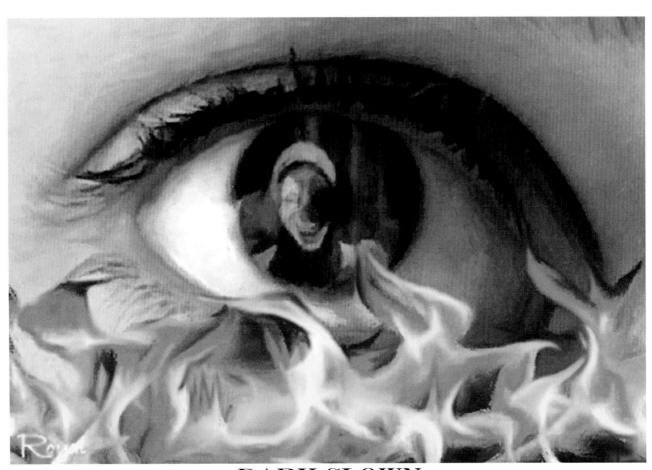

DARK CLOWN

JUST PERHAPS

ROYAL

MUD FLATS

THE SEDUCTION

COUNT FOSCO

MARY'S INK

SHADOW CABINET

LOST CITY OF Z

DIOGENES' RING

DOORWAY TO HELL

LIBERATION OF THE VILLE

THE RED METEOR

MIME

ELIXIR

Royal

SKIN WALKERS

INTO THE DEEP

MBWUN

MR. CAYUTE

KIVA

TWO MULES

FROM THE ISLE OF KUT

HOME INVADER

THE SURGEON'S END

SKULL CRUSHER ROCK

SMITHBACK AND CO.

SWEET MRS. KRAUS

A RELATIVE

GOODMAN LICKSPITTLE

SUDDEN IMPROVISATION

GASPARILLA

HIGHLAND MOORS

A WRITER'S SHED

PROFESSOR FROCK

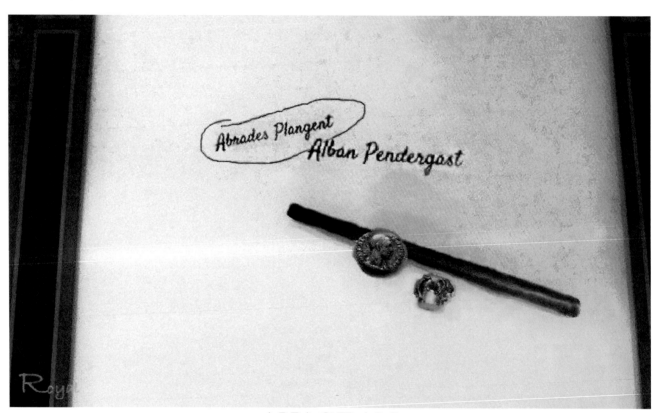

ANAGRAM

A BROTHER'S LOVE

"SUN !"

SHIFTED SANDS

CONSTANCE

THE GRAY REAPER

ENTER THE TOOTH FAIRY

SOUVENIRS

GREAT-AUNT CORNELIA

BRICK BY BRICK

LES BAER

QUEEQUEG

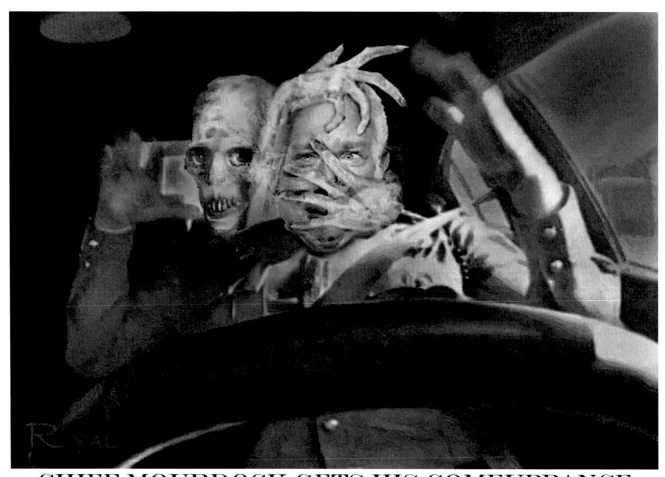

CHIEF MOURDOCK GETS HIS COMEUPPANCE

HEARTBREAK

THE GRAVE

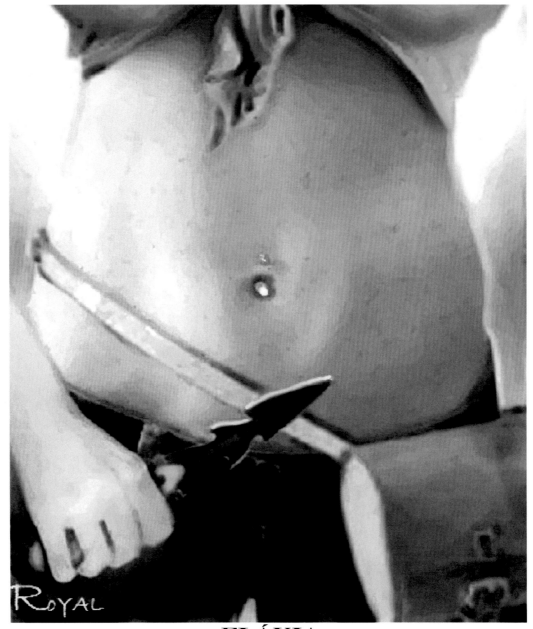

FLÁVIA

HIDDEN MANDALA

BRYCE IN THE RAMBLES

A STILL LIFE

THE PLACES WE'VE GONE

WAITING

RESURRECTION

ROYAL

URBAN ARCHEOLOGY

WHAT IS A MOON PIE ?

BLOODY FUR COAT

THE CASK OF AMONTILLADO

GRAPPLING

GREEN TANKA

THE RED LION

PRAYER STONES

THE NECROMANCER

HELEN'S REST

HUNTED

HOW DOES ONE EAT THIS?

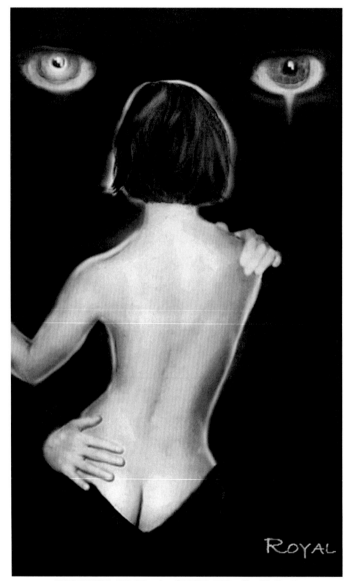

THE BLACK ROOM

Royal

STAND VERY STILL

AND YOU ARE?

PROFILE

SILVER WRATH

K-BAR

QUEEN'S QUORUM

ROULETTE

EARN YOUR M.R.E.

DETERMINATION

GREETINGS FROM MEDICINE CREEK

SOUND & LIGHT SHOW

THE GEM HEIST

BILLIARD BALLS

WRINKLER

UP FOR AIR

TRICK OR TREAT

TAPUI

BREEDERS

11764631R00080

Made in the USA
San Bernardino, CA
08 December 2018